THE
1980
U.S. OLYMPIC
BOYCOTT

A HISTORY PERSPECTIVES BOOK

Martin Gitlin

Published in the United States of America by Cherry Lake Publishing
Ann Arbor, Michigan
www.cherrylakepublishing.com

Consultants: Nicholas Evan Sarantakes, PhD, Associate Professor,
Department of Strategy and Policy, U.S. Naval War College; Marla Conn,
ReadAbility, Inc.
Editorial direction: Red Line Editorial
Book design and illustration: Sleeping Bear Press

Photo Credits: Barry Thumma/AP Images, cover (left), 1 (left); Tatiana
Popova/Shutterstock, cover (middle), 1 (middle); AP Images, cover (right),
1 (right), 4, 6, 14, 17, 18, 20, 23, 27, 28, 30; Michel Lipchitz/AP Images, 8;
Marty Lederhandler/AP Images, 12

Library of Congress Cataloging-in-Publication Data

Gitlin, Martin.
  The 1980 U.S. Olympic boycott / Martin Gitlin.
    pages cm -- (Perspectives library)
  ISBN 978-1-62431-663-0 (hardcover) -- ISBN 978-1-62431-690-6 (pbk.)
-- ISBN 978-1-62431-717-0 (pdf) -- ISBN 978-1-62431-744-6 (hosted
ebook)
  1. Olympic Games (22nd : 1980 : Moscow, Russia)--Juvenile literature. 2.
Olympics--Political aspects--Juvenile literature. 3. Sports and state--
United States. 4. Boycotts--United States. I. Title.

  GV7221980 .G57 2014
  796.48--dc23
                            2013029378

Cherry Lake Publishing would like to acknowledge the work of
The Partnership for 21st Century Skills. Please visit *www.p21.org*
for more information.

Printed in the United States of America
Corporate Graphics Inc.
January 2014

TABLE OF CONTENTS

In this book, you will read about the 1980 U.S. Olympic boycott from three perspectives. Each perspective is based on real things that happened to real people who were involved in or experienced the boycott. As you'll see, the same event can look different depending on one's point of view.

1

Vladimir Pilkov
Soviet Swimmer

Today, January 20, 1980, U.S. President Jimmy Carter gave an **ultimatum**. He demanded that our Soviet military leave Afghanistan by February 20. If we don't, the U.S. team will **boycott** the Summer Olympics here in Moscow. I understand the final decision to boycott will come from the United States Olympic Committee (USOC). It is the organization that makes decisions for the United States about participation in the Olympics. But I cannot imagine the USOC would go against the will of the president. And our government does not give in to threats. So it seems certain the Americans will stay home.

I follow politics quite closely. On December 24, 1979, Soviet troops marched into Afghanistan. Our leaders told us that it was to help the new **Communist** government there. But I don't fully believe that. Our government runs the media. So we usually don't get the full story. I believe we invaded the country to match the U.S. presence in nearby Pakistan. Our country also wants to get valuable oil in the Persian Gulf.

The invasion of Afghanistan has increased the tension between my country and the United States. The two countries have been battling to secure political and economic influence in the world since the end of World War II in 1945. My country has tried to convert other countries to Communism. The Americans seem to be deeply against Communism. They try to prevent it from spreading. The Americans want to make **capitalism** the top economic system. This period has been called a cold war between the two countries.

▲ *President Carter asked U.S. athletes to support the Olympic boycott.*

I might not always agree with the decisions my government makes. But I don't agree with this decision by the Americans. This is especially true when I think about 1936. That was the year **Nazi** Germany hosted the Summer Olympics. German dictator Adolf Hitler and his Nazi government were some of the most brutal leaders in history. The Americans knew the Nazis were mistreating the Jews of Germany. There were many people in the United States who wanted their country to boycott the Olympics. But the athletes participated. Nazi Germans eventually killed 6 million Jews during World War II. That is obviously much worse than what my country has done. U.S. athletes went to Nazi Germany. But they will not come to Moscow because we are in Afghanistan? It is outrageous.

Some people in my country believe being chosen to host the Olympics is in recognition of our good foreign policy. But the International Olympic

▲ *The Soviets claimed they were invited into Afghanistan by the country's government.*

Committee has told us Moscow was chosen for its athletic resources. No matter what, my country would never allow politics to ruin the Olympics. We have every intention of participating in the Winter Olympics in the United States next month even though the host country is threatening to boycott our event. We understand the Olympics should not be used for political reasons. The Olympics are meant to bring people together—not keep them apart. That is what Sergey Pavlov said in a speech last year. He is the chairman of the Soviet Committee of Physical Culture and Sport. He said our nation would prepare for the Summer Games with the idea that it is more than just athletes competing in various sports. He said the Soviet Union views hosting the Olympics as an opportunity to create bonds between the nations of the world. It is a beautiful idea. Now the United States is tearing it to shreds.

I think other capitalist countries will follow the United States' lead and join the boycott. The Americans have always had influence over their **allies** on moral

SECOND SOURCE

▶ Find another source that discusses the Soviets' beliefs about hosting the Olympics. Compare the information there with the information in this source.

SOVIETS LEAD THE GAMES

The host country, the Soviet Union, won the most medals at the 1980 Summer Olympics. The country won 195 overall, including 80 gold, to take first place in both categories. Communist countries under Soviet influence earned the top four spots in the Olympic standings.

issues. But the absence of those countries will not matter as much to me. The athletes I want to compete against come from the United States.

Some people might think I would be happy to have the Americans out of the Olympics. After all, they have the best male swimmers in the world. The United States won 12 of 13 gold medals in men's swimming at the 1976 Summer Games. The 1976 gold medalists John Hencken, Brian Goodell, and Mike Bruner are still on the U.S. team. If they don't come, I will have a better chance of winning a gold medal. But I would rather do it by competing against the best. If I do win a medal, I will still be incredibly happy, even if I don't compete against the Americans. Still, it is a shame the Americans will lose out on their chance to compete.

THINK ABOUT IT

▶ What is the main point of this chapter? Pick out two pieces of evidence that support your answer.

Richard Krantz

USOC Member

It is April 12, 1980. I just voted in favor of the United States boycotting the Summer Olympics. The USOC was responsible for deciding whether to allow the U.S. team to participate in the Moscow Games in July. We voted today by a 2–1 margin to boycott the Games.

The USOC works hard to be fair. We have always taken pride in our independent spirit.

We are like other Olympic committees around the world. We are proud of not being ruled by the wishes of our government. We could have voted for the boycott right after President Carter called for it three months ago. But we waited so we could think about the decision carefully. We wanted to take into account the opinion of the public. At this point, much of the public is in favor of the boycott.

We also took into account the opinion of Congress. The House of Representatives voted 386–12 to ban our team from competing in Moscow. The Senate followed with an 88–4 vote in favor of a boycott. Congress is not the body that decides whether our athletes boycott the games. But it was a powerful and symbolic vote. Still, many members of the USOC were on the fence. They were not eager to vote in favor of the boycott.

Then, two days ago, the president announced he would be prepared to take legal action to prevent

▲ *Much of the American public supported the Olympic boycott.*

U.S. athletes from competing in the Summer Games. How could the USOC vote to allow them to participate after that? Our duty to the athletes seemed to make it necessary to vote for the boycott in order to protect them from any possible legal trouble.

That knowledge did not make our task any easier. But I must admit that I personally believed voting for the boycott was the right thing to do—

even if President Carter hadn't called for it. I had to vote with my head and not with my heart. The United States must take a stand against the Soviet invasion of Afghanistan. If we had agreed to send our Olympic team to Moscow, we would be sending the wrong message to the Soviet leaders. We cannot allow one country to invade another with no good reason and get away with it. We had to punish them for their attack in a way that did not threaten military action. Politically, it made sense.

TROUBLE FOR TELEVISION

U.S. television network NBC spent two years planning their coverage of the 1980 Summer Olympics in Moscow. When the decision was made to boycott the games, the network lost a lot of money and planning.

ANALYZE THIS

▶ Analyze the first two narratives of the book. How are the perspectives of the Soviet athlete and the USOC member similar? How are they different?

Others on the USOC disagree with me. They voted against the boycott because they do not think politics should play a role in the Olympics. Of course, this would be ideal. But anyone who believes that is possible is foolish. In fact, boycotts or political demonstrations have played a role in a few of the past Olympics. Several countries boycotted the 1956 Games in Australia after the Soviets used military force to crush an anticommunist rebellion in Hungary. African-American track stars Tommie Smith and John Carlos raised their fists on the medal stand during the 1968 Summer Games in Mexico City, Mexico. They did this to call for African-American equality in the United States. Several African countries boycotted the 1976 Summer Games in Canada to protest the treatment of blacks in South Africa.

▲ *Tommie Smith, center, and John Carlos raised their fists in the air during their medal ceremony at the 1968 Summer Olympics.*

▲ *Vice President Mondale, right, spoke with the USOC president to try to convince him to support the boycott.*

....

Vice President Walter Mondale captured my thoughts perfectly. He spoke to the USOC before we voted today. He assured us that the president still supported the ideals of the Games. He added that President Carter hoped that in the future no nation would be allowed to serve as Olympic host while invading another, as the Soviets have done in Afghanistan.

I should be happy knowing that I did the right thing. But it is not that easy. We are now the enemies of every athlete that had earned a spot on the U.S. Olympic team. Maybe they have a right to feel that way. They sweat and toiled for a chance to compete against the greatest athletes in the world. Our vote, in essence, destroyed those dreams. I feel terrible for the athletes. I can only imagine how much it hurts to have their dreams shattered and to know all their hard work was in vain.

THINK ABOUT IT

▶ Read this chapter carefully. Determine its main point. Then pick out two pieces of evidence that support it.

Emily Robertson

U.S. Field Hockey Player

Do not misunderstand me. Competing for a gold medal in field hockey against the best teams in the world would have fulfilled a lifelong dream of mine. Traveling halfway around the world to experience new cultures would have been one of the greatest experiences of my life. I was angry and hurt when the boycott was first made official.

But after some time I took a step back and tried considering what was right for society. I was able to see the event with a different perspective. Now I am not so upset the United States boycotted the Summer Olympics in Moscow. I was disappointed that the athletes from England and France competed. They are two of our closest allies, and we should have all stood together. But 65 countries participated in the boycott, including Japan, West Germany, Canada, and China. That made me feel better.

Still, it is probably good that the U.S. television networks have decided not to air the Games. This would have been too painful for many athletes to watch. I know how the athletes are feeling here on July 28, 1980, while the games are still going on. I'm upset that we're not there competing too. I can even understand why 25 of our Olympic athletes filed a lawsuit against the USOC to overturn the boycott. I do not blame the U.S. Supreme Court for rejecting the lawsuit though.

SECOND SOURCE

▶ Find another source on the lawsuit filed by the 25 U.S. athletes against the U.S. government. Compare the information there to the information in this source.

I felt the same way as those athletes until I started looking at the global political picture. My cousin is one of the U.S. **hostages** who was seized in Iran on November 4, 1979. He is still being held captive. I showed my support for the hostages by tying a yellow ribbon around the tree in my front yard. But it does not look like we will be getting them back anytime soon.

The Iran hostage crisis has no tie to the Soviet invasion of Afghanistan. But knowing that my cousin is in such grave danger got me thinking that people must be held accountable for their actions. They must be punished if they take unfair actions or hurt others. Iran must be punished for supporting the taking of U.S. hostages. Similarly, the Soviet Union must be punished for invading Afghanistan. My recognition of that changed my view of the boycott.

My opinion has put me in direct conflict with some of my teammates. One of my best friends is a gymnast who felt she could have won a gold medal. She also said that if she had won gold, she could have achieved fame and fortune through marketing and advertising deals.

▲ *A gap is shown where British athletes would have marched during opening ceremonies. The athletes, who participated in Olympic events, did not participate in the opening ceremonies as a sign of protest.*

LAWSUIT

Twenty-five U.S. athletes sued the USOC to try to overturn the committee's decision to boycott the games. Anita DeFrantz was a U.S. rower. She was the lead name of the lawsuit. The athletes lost the lawsuit. DeFrantz later became the first U.S. woman to serve on the International Olympic Committee.

She is angry with me for not joining those who filed the lawsuit to overturn the boycott. I told her I used to feel the same way she did about the boycott. I was so mad. But now I support the boycott because I do think it was the right thing to do. My friend is looking only at what is good for her and her dreams. She is not thinking about what is good for the world.

The Soviet government curbs the freedom of its people. Their citizens cannot utter a word of protest or demonstrate against the war in Afghanistan if they think the Soviet invasion is wrong. If they did protest, they could wind up in jail or banished to the cold region of Siberia.

Perhaps my gymnast friend should learn about Andrei Sakharov. He is a famous Soviet scientist arrested for criticizing the government after the invasion. He has been **exiled** to the city of Gorky. Sakharov risked further punishment by supporting the boycott and even calling for the Games to be moved out of the Soviet Union. If Sakharov can put his life on the line, then my friend can accept the decision of the USOC.

What Sakharov is trying to do is bring freedom to his country. The Soviet government controls the media. Its people are told what the government wants them to know regarding why their military invaded

Afghanistan. But the people of the Soviet Union are surely noticing that 65 nations, including the United States, are boycotting the Moscow Olympics. Certainly they will question why the boycott is happening. Maybe they will question their government's actions too.

Looking at the boycott in this way should make my friend see that the boycott is bigger than any one athlete's dreams. But I do not mean to downplay their sadness and frustration. I can only imagine how Craig Beardsley is feeling right now. He is a swimmer from New Jersey who just set the world record in the 200-meter butterfly at the U.S. Nationals. His time was a second and a half faster than that of Sergei Fesenko of the Soviet Union, who just won that same event at the Olympics in Moscow. Beardsley must believe he was cheated out of that gold medal. I do not blame him.

I think about the U.S. men's hockey team's stunning performance at the Winter Olympics in February. It shocked the Soviets by defeating them and reaching the finals. Afterward, the U.S. team won the gold medal. The U.S. team defeating the Soviets was considered one of the greatest upsets in sports

▲ *Sergei Fesenko of the Soviet Union won the Olympic gold medal in the 200-meter butterfly.*

▲ *The U.S. hockey team celebrated after winning the gold medal at the 1980 Winter Games.*

history. After all, these were a bunch of college kids beating one of the greatest hockey teams in the world. It was an achievement those U.S. hockey players will cherish for the rest of their lives.

Not one U.S. athlete had a chance to experience that joy in the Summer Olympics. That is such a shame. But not as big a shame as it would have been had we gone to Moscow and failed to protest the invasion of Afghanistan. This boycott might not be fair. But it is the right thing to do.

ANALYZE THIS

▶ Analyze the perspectives of the Soviet athlete and the U.S. athlete. How are they similar? How are they different?

LOOK, LOOK AGAIN

This photo shows President Carter asking athletes on the U.S. Olympic team to support his proposed boycott. Use this image to answer the following questions:

1. How would a Soviet athlete describe this event to his fellow athletes?

2. How would a USOC member react to this event?

3. What would a U.S. athlete in the audience be thinking as he or she listened to President Carter?

GLOSSARY

allies (AL-eyes) countries that are on the same side during a war or disagreement

boycott (BOI-kaht) to refuse to buy goods or participate in something as a form of protest

capitalism (KAP-i-tuh-liz-uhm) an economic system in which most property belongs to individuals rather than the government

Communist (KOM-yuh-nist) referring to an economic and political system in which the government owns most property and controls the means of production

exiled (EG-zyld) sent away from a country, usually for political reasons

hostages (HAH-sti-jes) people who are kept prisoner by others who demand something in order for the people to be released

Nazi (NAHT-see) a member of the National Socialist German Workers' Party, which ruled Germany from 1933 to 1945

ultimatum (uhl-tuh-MAY-tuhm) a final demand that carries the threat of punishment if ignored

LEARN MORE

Further Reading

Adams, Simon. *The Cold War*. North Mankato, MN: Sea-to-Sea, 2004.
Bachrach, Susan D. *The Nazi Olympics: Berlin 1936*. Boston: Little, Brown, 2000.
Macy, Sue. *Swifter, Higher, Stronger: A Photographic History of the Summer Olympics*. Washington, DC: National Geographic, 2008.

Web Sites

Cold War
http://www.history.com/topics/cold-war
This Web site has information about the Cold War, which played a role in the 1980 U.S. Olympic boycott.

Moscow 1980
http://www.olympic.org/moscow-1980-summer-olympics
This Web site has information about the 1980 U.S. Olympic boycott as well as results and photos of the Games.

INDEX

ABOUT THE AUTHOR

Martin Gitlin is a freelance writer based in Cleveland, Ohio. He has had about 70 educational books published, including many about American history. He has won more than 45 writing awards, including first place for General Excellence from the Associated Press.